This book is dedic:
"Bras de Fer" and T......... Bjorn "Ironside"

The author of this book Benjamin James Baillie lives
and works in Normandy

THE GREAT HEATHEN ARMY

Ivar "the Boneless" and the Viking invasion of Britain

865 - 878 AD

By Benjamin James Baillie

Contents

Introduction

In 865 AD a huge Viking army appeared out of the mists of the North Sea from Scandinavia and landed on the East Anglian coast. Their objective was nothing less than the total conquest of Anglo-Saxon England and the whole of the British Isles. Numbering some 10,000 to 15,000 men the "Great Heathen Army" was the largest invasion force since Roman Legions had landed on the shores of Britannia back in 43 AD. During a 14 year reign of terror they left a brutal trail of destruction in their wake. At its head the army was led by the vengeful sons of the Viking adventurer, Ragnar Lodbrok "Hairy breeches". The mastermind behind the invasion became one of the most feared and cruel warlords of the Viking age, Ivar "the Boneless". His shadow cast a dark cloud over the British Isles that ultimately led to the unification and creation of the nation state of England.

The coming of the Northmen 789 – 865 AD

In 789 AD the Anglo-Saxon chronicle reported one of the first Viking raids on the British Isles. Three dragon head longships from Hordaland in Norway landed on the Isle of Portland (Wessex coastline, near modern day Dorchester). They were approached by the local reeve, Beaduheard (Royal official) who had mistaken them for merchants. He compelled them to follow him to the Royal manor, but they immediately slew him on the spot before returning to their ships and disappearing onto the horizon. This incident was the first in a series of bloody raids inflicted on Europe by the Northmen from Scandinavia.

In 792 AD King Offa of Mercia began to make defensive measures against the seaborne raids from the North. Just one year later the Vikings struck again in a raid that epitomised their lust for blood and booty. The attack just off the Northumbrian

Holy Island, Lindisfarne

coastline on the holy Island of Lindisfarne shocked the courts of Western Europe. The Northmen attacked one of holiest places in Anglo Saxon England, the monastery of St Aidan and Cuthbert. Striking with surprise, speed and extreme aggression the monks on the Island were taken by complete surprise and overwhelmed immediately.

The raiders began their work of bloody destruction, looting the monastery of its gold and silver and slaughtering the defenceless monks. After a few hours they returned to their longships laden down with the rich spoils of the raid, which also included a valuable human commodity; slaves. Behind them lay a scene of utter carnage: burning buildings lit up the Northumbrian sky, the monastery high altar was left broken and spattered with blood and precious books and manuscripts littered the courtyard amongst the bodies of the innocent.

The Anglo Saxon chronicle:

In this year of 793 AD fierce, foreboding omens came over the land of the Northumbrians, the ravaging of wretched heathen people destroyed God's church at Lindisfarne.

Lindisfarne carving depicting the Viking raid of 793 AD

In 794 AD raiders this time from Denmark returned, but were wiped out by a Northumbrian defence force near Jarrow. According to the Anglo-Saxon chronicle they were harassed by bad weather, possibly making their usual quick gateway near impossible. The raiding party was annihilated and their King put to death in a cruel manner.

The Vikings secret weapon was their Longships. These vessels could cross the open seas and also sail up the shallowest of rivers with ease. With no standing army and over 5000 miles of coastline to protect it was impossible for the independent English Kingdoms to combat the Viking menace.

In 835 AD the Northmen ravaged the Isle of Sheppey and the Thames estuary. The following year near Carhampton (Somerset) King Egbert of Wessex fought a pitched battle against the crews of some thirty five ships. Using the famous Gokstad Ship discovered in Vestfold, Southern Norway as an indication marker, Egbert would have been facing a force of some 2000 Vikings. Whatever the exact size of the invading force it was large enough to defeat the Saxon King on this occasion. Egbert revenged the defeat by smashing a second Viking attack in the West Country at Hingston Down, 838 AD. This time the Vikings had allied themselves with the semi-autonomous Cornish Britons of Dunmonia (Cornwall). The defeat in the Tamar valley caused the Cornish to begrudgingly accept the over lordship of King Egbert and the West Saxons of Wessex.

It may also have been the start in the change of Viking tactics. Initially the raids consisted of a small number of ships acting independently, but from the 830s onwards the Northmen were banding together and creating huge mobile raiding fleets.

Over population, the rise of central authority, dynastic squabbles, lack of arable land and a fierce spirit of adventure were amongst some of the reasons why the Vikings were venturing out on expeditions of exploration and conquest.

Using their trading networks to gather information on the situation in the British Isles and on the continent, the Vikings were able to select which country or region to attack with the greatest chance of success.

The St Alban flag attributed to the Anglo-Saxon Kingdom of Mercia

Over the next 35 years the attacks increased in ferocity and size. In 841 AD Lindsey (Lincolnshire) and East Anglia was penetrated by the heathens, followed by the ravaging of London and Rochester in 842 AD. A more disturbing pattern took place in 850 AD when a Viking army did not leave at the end of the raiding season; instead they fortified themselves on the Isle of Thanet and over wintered there. They were then reinforced by a fleet of 350 ships during the following spring.

This huge force disembarked on the Kentish coast and stormed Canterbury and London. The Vikings put to flight the Mercian army of King Beorhtwulf and terrorised the region, ransacking the churches and villages within the vicinity. In the meantime King Athelwulf (Egbert's son) had raised the Wessex field army and confronted the invaders at Aclea, probably modern-day Oakley Green (Berkshire) near the river Thames.

Anglo-Saxon Chronicle recorded that:

"350 ships came into the Thames and attacked Canterbury, London and put to flight Beorhtwulf, King of Mercia with his army, and then went south over the Thames into Surrey. King Aethelwulf and his son Aethelbald with the West Saxon army fought against them at Oak Field Aclea, and there made the greatest slaughter of a heathen army that we have heard tell of up to the present day, and there took the victory."

The Anglo-Saxon victory at Aclea destroyed the Viking land force and was swiftly followed up by one of the first recorded naval victories in English history. According to the Anglo-Saxon chronicle Athelstan (the King's eldest son) and Earlorman Ealhhere fought in ships and slew the heathens at Sandwich in Kent, they captured nine longships and put the others to flight.

Norse Viking raiders from an early medieval manuscript

Although defeated, the Northmen returned in force and wintered on the Isle of Sheppey in 855 AD. Just as in Ireland, Scotland and on the continent the Vikings were creating bases by fortifying Islands or constructing "Longports" to enable them to strike at will, undermine Royal authority and extract the "Danegeld" protection money from the surrounding region. On man stands out as the archetypical Viking warlord of the raiding age, his name is Ragnar Lodbrok "Hairy breeches".

Raganar Lodbrok "Hairy breeches

Ragnar's fame was legendary, and his exploits earned him a place as one of the most popular heroes in the Viking Sagas. Although his genealogy as far from clear, according to the Icelandic Sagas Ragnar was the only son of Sigurd Hring, one time King of Sweden and Denmark.

Ragnar Lodbrok Saga:

"Ragnar was a large man, fair in appearance and with good intelligence, generous with his men, but stern with his enemies"

On reaching adulthood Ragnar married Ipora, the daughter of Earl Herrud of whom he had two sons with, Erik and Agnar. When Ipora died from an illness Ragnar equipped himself with ships, warriors and set out on a career of raiding. Ragnar's most famous raid took place in 845 AD. His Viking fleet of 120 longboats sailed the 240 miles from the sea to the French capital Paris. After ravaging the city of Rouen his pagan war band continued upstream and sacked the modern day town of Chaussy near Paris.

The new French King, Charles II "the bald" raised an army and set out to confront Ragnar's Vikings. He split his army on either side of the Seine River hoping to encircle the Norsemen, but Ragnar realised what Charles was up to and quickly ambushed the smaller Frankish force, taking numerous prisoners and slaughtering the rest.

The 111 prisoners were then executed on a tiny island in the middle of the Seine in front of Charles's second force. In a ferocious frenzy, the Vikings launched a second attack against the remainder of the French forces. Charles fearing for his life fled the scene with the remnants of his army and headed for the safety of St Denis.

With the French forces destroyed, Ragnar terrorized the region, sacking

King Charles II "the bald"

towns, villages and wasting the land. On Easter Sunday 845 A.D the Vikings broke through the defences of the island city of Paris and plundered the capital.

Ragnar "Lodbrok"

Charles who was still in St Denis behind the Vikings could have blocked off the Seine River and any escape route open to them. Instead he hesitated, and paid Ragnar off with 7000 pounds of silver. Charles payment became known as the "Dane geld" (Danes pay) or simply, protection money to stop any further aggression. The marauding Norsemen returned back down the river Seine to Scandinavia unmolested.

The Saekonungar: Ragnar's sons

Ragnar married a second time to a beautiful young maiden by the name of Kraka (also called Aslaug). On their wedding night Ragnar wanted to consummate the marriage, but Kraka warned him of an evil prophecy.

Ragnar Saga:

> **"Three nights shall thus pass,**
> **Apart in the evening, although settled together in one**
> **hall, before our sacrifice to the gods: thus shall this**
> **denial prevent a lasting harm to my son- he whom you**
> **are hasty to beget will have no bones"**

Ragnar gave no heed to Kraka's prophecy and forced himself on her. Kraka knew herself to be with child and in time she gave birth to a boy. The baby was sprinkled with water and given the name Ivar. The prophecy came true and Ivar was born boneless, there was only gristle and cartilage where his bones should have been. More sons followed including Bjorn "Ironside", Hvitserk/Halfdan "the Wide embrace", Sigurd "Snake in the eye", Ubba and Rognavald.

Although Ivar seems to have been born with a disability and had to use staves during his childhood, this in no way impeded his position as Ragnar's eldest son and heir. Indeed according to the Sagas all his brothers respected his advice wherever they went. The Ragnarssons followed their father into a career of raiding and piracy. Ivar asked his father to supply him and his brothers with men and ships to which Ragnar gladly agreed.

Ivar:

"Now I want us to want to have ships prepared for us, and troops enough to man them, and then I want us to gain gold for ourselves"

The Ragnarssons embarked on a brutal series of campaigns in Scandinavia and Europe. Their fame even started to eclipse Ragnar who became jealous with envy. In one of the greatest Viking raids of the age they ventured south raiding France and then onto the Iberian Peninsula. After crossing the straits of Gibraltar the Northmen raided the Balearic Islands and then wintered in the Camargue region of Southern France. The Old Roman towns of Nimes and Arles were attacked and for many of the Scandinavians it would have been the first time that they would have seen the monumental stone buildings such as the Maison Carrée and the Arènes de Nîmes (Roman amphitheatre) relics from a former time of imperial Roman splendor.

The following spring the fleet set sail and attacked the coast of Italy, sacking Pisa and then advancing onto Luna, which they believed to be Rome. In a cunning plan they faked the death of one of their leaders (Bjorn "Ironside) and asked the leading citizens and clergy of Luna if they would permit him to be laid to rest in the City's Cathedral.

Maison Carrée, Nîmes, Southern France

Eager to have the body interned in the city out of hope of future patronage and pilgrims, the leading burgers of Luna agreed. The unarmed Viking pall bearers carried the coffin along the procession route and upon reaching the City's gates they jammed the entrance open using it.

At this very moment the supposedly dead leader Bjorn burst out of the coffin very much alive and handed his compatriots weapons hidden alongside him. Bjorn's men overwhelmed the guards protecting the entrance to the city and let the whole Viking army inside. Luna was ransacked by the Northmen and reduced to a burning heap of ruble. This same tactic was again used by one of the last Vikings: Harald "Hardrada" during the 1038 AD Byzantine campaign in Sicily and again by Robert Guiscard, the Norman Conqueror of Southern Italy and Sicily. Coincidently Robert Guiscard was descended from Rollo's Norwegian Vikings who settled down in Northern Western France creating the Duchy of Normandy in the early 10th century.

On their way back home they fought off an attempt by the Muslim Emir of Cordoba to destroy the fleet in retaliation for their earlier raids on Lisbon, Cadiz and Seville. The Northmen also captured several African slaves called 'blámenn', (blue men) in Norse. These unfortunate soles ended up in the slave market in Dublin, possibly taken their by Ivar who was also the co-ruler of the Viking colony along with Olaf the White.

The death of Ragnar Lodbrok

With his sons active in Scandinavia, Ireland and continental Europe Ragnar was eager to regain the limelight and seal his place in history as the greatest Viking adventurer of the age. He decided to raid England for one last time with only two ships. According to the Sagas he told his wife Randalin (possibly another name for Aslaug)

"There is no glory if men conquer a land with many ships, but there is no tale of anyone who has conquered England with two ships"

On route to England Ragnar's ships were caught in a violent storm and shipwrecked on the Northumbrian coastline. In a brief skirmish he was captured by the Northumbrian King Ælla. As a punishment for attacking his Kingdom Ælla had Ragnar thrown into a pit of snakes and bitten to death. As the snakes bit deep into Ragnar's flesh, he laughed at his captors and acclaimed:

"The young pigs would squeal if they knew the state of the old boar; of the injury beset onto me. Snakes dig into my flesh, stab at me harshly and have sucked on me; soon now will my body die among the beasts"

Messengers from King Ælla brought the news of Ragnar's death to his sons in Denmark. As they entered the great hall the Ragnarssons were feasting and reveling. Ivar sat in Ragnar's empty seat and invited the messengers to come forward and give their tidings. As the story of Ragnar's end unfolded, Halfdan who was playing chess with Sigurd crushed the chess piece in his hand so tightly that blood spurted out. Bjorn grabbed a spear shaft and pressed into it so strongly that he left his imprint in the wood. Sigurd who was cutting his nails with a knife, cut deep into his hand, right to the bone.

Viking invasion fleet from St Edmund's manuscript

Their rage was boiling over with anger, Halfdan ordered the messengers to be put to death on the spot, but Ivar intervened and allowed them to return to England with the message that he wanted King Ælla to give him as much land as an oxe hide covers.

When the envoys returned back to the Northumbian court they told King Ælla that Ivar meant him no harm and only wanted some land compensation for the death of Ragnar. Ælla had been fooled and Ivar "the Boneless" began to hatch a cold blooded plan not only to avenge his father's death, but also to subdue the whole of the British Isles.

The Great Heathen army's invasion of England 865 AD

Ivar "the Boneless" now the head of the formidable Ragnarsson clan gathered together a large coalition of Viking warlords under his father's sacred raven banner. The objective of the fore coming campaign was to conquer and settle the Island of Britannia. The Anglo-Saxon Kingdoms of England would face the initial Viking onslaught. Out of the fog of the North Sea Ivar's massive fleet of some 10,000-15,000 battle hardened Norsemen landed on the East Anglian shore. East Anglia may have been chosen for strategic reasons, being a much smaller Kingdom than that of Northumbria, Mercia and Wessex. It would have been unable to resist the Great Heathen Army without help from the neighbouring Anglo-Saxon Kingdoms. Also it may have been an easier rendezvous point for the Viking contingents coming from Frisia and the other parts of continental Europe.

The Conquest of Northumbria 866 AD

The East Anglian landings fooled King Ælla that he was not the target of Viking aggression. Ivar's heathen host spread out across the land and forced the King of East Anglia, Edmund to negotiate and provide the Vikings with horses and provisions.

Ivar and the army wintered in East Anglia and gathered intelligence on events in Northumbria. All was not well in the Northern Kingdom for King Ælla was in the midst of a civil war with Osbert, another contender for the Northumbrian crown. With the Northumbrians divided, Ivar "the Boneless" decided the time was right to launch a surprise attack.

Carefully choosing the Christian festival of the 1st of November (All saints day) 866 AD for the attack, Ivar advanced from East Anglia over the river Humber towards his target: York, the greatest city in Northern England.

Using the horses obtained from King Edmund, the speed and surprise combined with the Christian holy day allowed Ivar to take the city with virtually no resistance. Once secured, Ivar decided to make York (Jorvik in Old Norse) his capital and base. The city was ideally placed on the river Ouse, allowing supplies and reinforcements to reach it from the North Sea with ease. It also had the extra advantage of having extensive Roman defensive walls surrounding the city. Ivar ordered his men to repair any weaknesses in the Roman walls and prepare for the Anglo-Saxon assault which he knew would be forcoming.

King Ælla and King Osbert put their differences aside and gathered together an immense army to regain York from the heathens. Ivar and his brothers watched the Northumbrians advance towards the city from the battlements. They encouraged their men with the battle cries to avenge Ragnar and destroy the men of the White Christ. Viking horns sounded a frightening noise towards the advancing Northumbrians, spreading fear through their ranks

The Northumbrian assault managed to penetrate the city's fortifications, but once inside they were met with a fierce counter attack by the blood thirsty Vikings. Ivar ordered his fearless berserkers to spearhead the Viking attack.

These religious fanatics fought with an uncontrollable fury, believing that if they died in battle they would enter Valhalla (the Viking Heaven) and be at the side of Odin at the Ragnarak. As Ivar's berserkers pushed back the Northumbrians, the tide began to turn in favour of the defenders. The battle raged on, inside and on the Roman walls. Finally the Northumbrians were driven out of the city with heavy loses and then slaughter began.

King Osbert was slain in the thickest press and with his death Northumbrian resistance crumbled. King Ælla was beaten to the ground and taken alive in the vicious hand to hand combat. With their leaders dead or in captivity the remaining Northumbrians fled the bloody field in panic and disorder.

The Roman/medieval walls of York

Ivar "The Boneless"

The unfortunate King Ælla was brought before Ivar, Sigurd, Halfdan and Bjorn. The brothers had waited a long time to avenge the murder of their father. Ivar sentenced Ælla to death according to the tradition of the blood eagle (A cruel Viking method of torture and execution). The Skaldic poem Knutsdrapa translated that Ælla had his back cut open and his lungs pulled out from his ribs to form a pair of wings. This was all done while Ælla was still breathing.

Now leaderless, Northumbrian resistance crumbled in the face of the Great Heathen Army. Ivar let loose his marauding Norsemen in a brutal reign of terror; villages, farms and settlements were destroyed and razed to the ground in order to sustain the army and also to strike fear into anyone who had ideas of defying their new Northern masters: the Vikings.

Simeon de Durham stated:

"The army raided here there and filled every place with bloodshed and sorrow. Far and wide it destroyed the churches and monasteries with fire and sword. When it departed from a place it left nothing standing but roofless walls. So great was the destruction that even now one can scarcely see anything left of those places, nor any sign of their former greatness"

Blood eagle execution from a Viking stone carving

Testing the defences: Merica 868 AD

With Northumbria subdued Ivar set up Egbert (a Northumbrian nobleman) as his puppet King on the Northumbrian throne. Mercia had been the strongest of the Anglo-Saxon Kingdoms, but after the death of King Offa in 796 AD and his son Cenwulf in 821 AD Wessex became the dominant Kingdom in England. Using the onset of winter and the harvest as cover, Ivar stormed south and captured Nottingham in late 868 AD. Nottingham's strategic position on the high ground above the River Trent allowed Ivar to test the defences of Mercia. King Burgred of Mercia refused to fight the Vikings alone and sent for help from King Aethelred of Wessex and his brother Alfred (later King Alfred the Great). The combined Anglo-Saxon armies of Wessex and Mercia converged on Nottingham for a final showdown with Ivar's Great Heathen Army.

Ivar possibly outnumbered refused to give up his defensive position and dug in for the winter. Likewise the Anglo-Saxons were not prepared for either a risky direct assault on the Viking defences of the city or a long drawn out siege.

In the end according to the Norman Chronicler Henry de Huntington:

"Ivar then, seeing that the whole of England was there gathered, and that his host was weaker betook himself to smooth words – Like a cunning fox he won peace and returned back to York, where he ruled for one year with great cruelty"

The peace terms agreed at Nottingham allowed Ivar to vacate the city without any interference from the Anglo-Saxons and return to York unmolested. Merica's alliance with Wessex had thwarted his plan to annex the Middle Anglo-Saxon Kingdom for the time being, but it also accelerated his plan to destroy East Anglia.

St Edmund and the destruction of East Anglia 869 AD

Ivar then planned the next campaign move. The Anglo-Saxon Kingdom of East Anglia was the next target of Viking aggression. Ivar had inside knowledge of King Edmund and the Saxon Kingdom during the over wintering at Thetford in 865 AD. East Anglia had once been one of the most important and powerful Kingdoms during the 7th century under King Rædwald of the Wuffingas dynasty, but its power had been superseded by Mercia, Northumbria and Wessex in the centuries that followed.

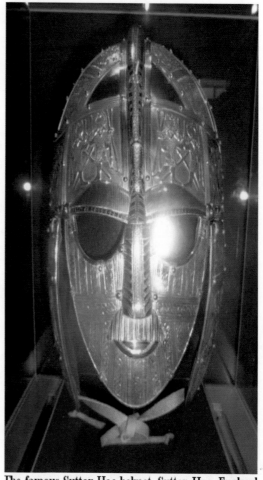

The famous Sutton Hoo helmet, Sutton Hoo, England

Its North Sea coastline was strategically important to Ivar as the fall of East Anglia would mean that the Vikings would control all the major ports and towns from the river Tyne in the North to the Thames estuary in the south. The Kingdom's military weakness compared to its neighbours made East Anglia to prefect target for conquest.

Ivar sent envoy's to King Edmund who was at his manor at Hoxle. The message was blunt and simple; submit and acknowledge Ivar as his overlord, renounce the White Christ (Christianity) and convert to paganism or face the total destruction of the Kingdom.
When Edmund received the message he at once refused the offer and declared:

"A Christian King had no such love of his life on Earth that he would submit to a pagan Lord"

What Edmund did not know was that Ivar had already anticipated such a response and had launched his invasion of East Anglia in earnest. As Edmund sent out commissions of array, Viking troops were already advancing by land through Mercia and across the Wash estuary.
The Heathens overran the Kingdom destroying everything in their wake. At Peterborough they looted and burned the town to the ground along with killing the Abbot and his monks. King Edmund was taken by complete surprise when his spies bought back word that the Vikings were within a few miles of his manor at Hoxne. At the battle of Haegelisdun (probably near Bradfield St Clare) the Anglian forces were routed and annihilated.
Like King Ælla before him Edmund was taken alive and brought before Ivar and the Ragnarsson brothers. Ivar had

the proud young King beaten in front of him and his brothers. He was then bound to a tree where his captors mocked him and shot his body full of arrows.

As the life drained out of his body, Ivar had one last act of cruelty to bestow on King Edmund; finally his head was struck off and slung onto the woodland floor.

Legend has it that some of the surviving Anglian soldiers retrieved the King's head from between the paws of a giant wolf.

Medieval manuscript depicting the death of King Edmund of East Anglia by the Vikings

It was then laid to rest in Beodrices-Weorth which in time became known as Bury St Edmunds. Ivar's lightening campaign and the brutal murder of King Edmund had cleared another chess piece off the board. The East Anglian Kingdom which had been founded by the Angles after the Roman withdrawal in the 5th century ceased to exist as an independent Kingdom. Ivar was not interested in a total dismantlement of the Anglian state, as soon as the local resistance was extinguished, he over wintered at Thetford and installed Oswald as his puppet King.

Ubba Ragnarsson

Ivar's conquest of the Rock of Dunbarton

With virtually the entire of Eastern England under his control, Ivar returned to York and embarked on another campaign to subdue Northern Britain. As Olaf the White (Ivar's co-ruler in Dublin) crossed the Irish Sea, Ivar advanced from York overland into the ancient British Kingdom of Strathclyde. Stretching from Loch Lomond in the central belt of Scotland in the north to Cumbria in modern day England, Strathclyde was strategically important in controlling the Irish Sea and linking up with the newly conquered Viking colony of Northumbria. The Capital of Strathclyde lay on the river Clyde and was known as Dun Breatann "fortress of the Britons". The impregnable rock, (Dunbarton Rock) had been the centre of Brythonic power for over 400 years. Rising some 240 feet above the river it dominated the area and presented a formidable task for any would-be invader.

The two pronged Viking attack from land and sea caused panic in the Kingdom. Refugees were flooding to the capital trying to escape the advancing Vikings. When Ivar and Olaf's dragon head ships arrived in the Clyde outside the Rock of Dunbarton, it was clear that a direct assault would be suicidal. Ever the master of cunning and deceit Ivar laid siege to the rock, cutting off its supplies of fresh water and food. The Vikings tightened their grip around the Kingdom, raiding parties were sent out to terrorise the local inhabitants and gather up supplies for the siege. When the well in the citadel ran dry the defenders could no longer endure the daily horror of the siege. After four months King Artgal Mac Dumnagual finally surrendered the citadel to Ivar and Olaf. The Vikings ransacked Dunbarton and took a large number of Angles, Britons and Picts captive.

Annals of Ulster:
"Ivar and Olaf besieged Alcluith (Dunbarton), pillaged and razed it to the ground"

They over wintered in Strathclyde before setting sail back to Dublin with over 200 ships full of booty and prisoners including King Artgal. Once back in Dublin the hapless captives were sold off into slavery. Many were to go on and lead a miserable life in Scandinavia and even as far off as Muslim controlled North Africa.
Ivar held King Artgal to ransom, sending the demands for his release to Rhin his son and to the King of early Scotland, (Constantine I.) In a ruthless age Constantine I sent back a message to Ivar and Olaf. He would pay the ransom on condition that Argal was put to death. With Artgal out the way he could marry off his sister to Artgal's son, thus placing his own puppet on the throne of

Strathclyde and annexing it into the emerging Kingdom of Scotland. Ivar agreed, and upon receipt of the payment Artgal was murdered in cold blood. For the next two years Ivar ruled over the various Viking factions in Ireland, while his ally Olaf "the White" took ship back to Scotland and continued carving out a Viking Kingdom that stretched from Ireland all the way back to Vestfold in Norway. In 873 AD according to the Irish annals the most cruel and invincible Ivar "the Boneless" died a peaceful death in Dublin.

Annals of Ulster:
"873 AD Ivar, King of all the Northmen of all Ireland and Britain died"

Into Wessex, the year of the nine battles 870-871 AD

Back in England Ivar's brothers Halfdan and Ubba had been given the task of subduing the remaining Anglo-Saxon Kingdoms (Wessex and Mercia). On a frosty morning in late December 870 AD the dawn tranquility was abruptly scattered by the sound of horses' hooves and footsteps of the battle hardened warriors of the Great Heathen Army: the Vikings were on the move again. This time with extreme speed and surprise, the pagans thundered over the East Anglian border into Wessex. Halfdan and Ubba set up a fortified base at Reading in Berkshire where the rivers Thames and Thanet converge. This fortification was well placed to attack the heartland of Wessex and also to be re-supplied if necessary from Viking controlled East Anglia via the river Thames or overland using the old Roman road of Icknield way.

According to the Anglo-Saxon chronicle, two Danish Jarls rode out from the main Viking camp to raid the Berkshire countryside and gather up supplies. At Englefield they were confronted by Ealdorman Ethelwulf and the local Saxon fryd. In the ensuing battle one of the Danish Jarls, Sidrac was killed. With confusion rife in the Viking lines Ethelwulf hammered home the Saxon victory, forcing the remaining pagans to retreat back to their fortified camp.

Fresh from success and with the arrival of the main Wessex army under King Aethelred and his brother Prince Alfred, the West Saxons decided to attack the fortified Viking camp. The men of Wessex stormed the ramparts and slaughtered all the Vikings outside the main defences, but Halfdan and Ubba counterattacked with great ferocity and forced the Saxons to abandon the assault. Ealdman Ethelwulf who had won the first victory against the invaders just days earlier was cut down and killed outside the gates of the Viking fortification.

The Battle of Ashdown 871 AD

Halfdan rallied the "Great Heathen Army" and gave chase to King Aethelred's retreating troops. The West Saxons withdrew to the high ground of the Ridgeway, where King Aethelred sent out summons of array for reinforcements to join him. Viking scouts returned to Reading and reported that the West Saxons were rallying near the ancient chalk stone carving of the white horse by Uffington. With momentum now with the Vikings and only needing one decisive victory to extinguish the Kingdom of Wessex once and for all Halfdan ordered his men to march out of Reading towards the Ridgeway. Just four days after the Battle of Reading the two armies confronted each other once again at a place called "Ashdown".

As dawn broke on the morning of the 8th of January 871 AD the fog lifted to reveal a menacing sight on the ridge above the West Saxon camp. Aligned along the crest of the hill with the guðfani raven banner fluttering in the cold wind was the "Great Heathen Army". They had used horses and ponies for speed to arrive at the higher ground and take the West Saxons by surprise. The pagans were drawn up into two divisions, Kings Halfdan and Bagsecg commanding one and the other led by a collection of Viking Jarls. King Aethelred quickly reacted and mirrored the Viking formations, splitting the fryd in two. He led his contingent against Kings Halfdan and Bagsecg while Prince Alfred was tasked with confronting the Viking Jarls division.

Prince Alfred impatiently ordered his division to advance while the King was still attending mass in his royal tent. King Aethelred quickly returned to the front line encouraging his own men forward. As Alfred's men made their way up the sloop of the hill carrying the sacred Wyern banner of Wessex, they were met with the wild battle cries and howling of the pagans. The deafening noise grew louder as the heathens banged their weapons against their shields. For the inexperienced soldiers of the fryd this must have been a stomach churning moment, but the stakes were high and defeat meant certain death and slavery for their families. As the armies neared one another, the Viking commanders ordered a general charge, hoping to use the momentum of the sloop to break through the West Saxon shield wall.

The pagans smashed into Alfred's division first, causing the West Saxon shield wall to reel back from the initial charge. Prince Alfred led by example, striking back and cutting deep into the Viking ranks. His court chronicler

Asser later recalled:

"Alfred finally deployed the Christian forces against the heathens, even though the King had not yet joined him. Acting like a wild boar, supported by divine help, he closed up the shield wall and moved his army against the Danes".

Only when King Aethelred's division joined the battle were the West Saxons able to slowly push back the pagans. The hand to hand combat was unrelenting with friend and foe butchered on the blood soaked field of Ashdown. The battle raged on around a lone thorn tree with both sides swaying back and forward during the course of the day. The deadlock was finally broken when the Viking King Bagsecg was slain. His death along with five Danish Jarls (Sidroc the older and younger, Harald, Osbern and Freana) finally ended the day in favour of King Aethelred and Prince Alfred. As nightfall fell on the bloody field, Halfdan ordered and general retreat back to the Viking encampment at Reading. This was the first time the "Great Heathen Army" had suffered defeat since their arrival on the shores of Britannia back in 865 AD. Although bloodied they were not by any means decisively defeated.

The Battles of Old Basing and Meretun/Marten 871 AD

Only two weeks after the defeat at Ashdown, Halfdan felt strong enough to lead the army out of Reading in a bold march towards the capital of Wessex, Winchester. King Aethelred and Prince Alfred caught up with the "Great Heathen Army" who had entrenched themselves near the village of Old Basing on the banks on the River Loddon, within only a day's striking distance from Winchester.

King Aethelred took the decision to mount an assault on the fortified position, believing that the heathen's strength had been greatly reduced after the Battle of Ashdown.

He was greatly mistaken; Halfdan's men repulsed the West

Saxon attack with great slaughter, forcing them to flee the field. Both sides had sustained heavy casualties during the previous engagements and a lull ensued.

King Aethelred and Alfred were only able to mount a fresh offensive in late March. At Meretun near Marlborough in the heart of Wessex the two armies squared up to one another once again. Just like at Ashdown the battle raged on all day with both sides attacking and then counter attacking. This time it was the West Saxons who lost men of high rank, including Bishop Heahmund of Sherbourne, who was cut down in the fighting. King Aethelred may also have been injured in the battle. The Vikings prevailed and Prince Alfred and the King broke off the engagement and retired to safety with the remaining Wessex forces.

The arrival of the Great Summer Army 871 AD

Shortly after Easter, King Aethelred died. The Witan council of Wessex immediately elected Alfred as successor to the throne. Alfred's task was to fight on and defeat the Vikings at all costs, but shattering news arrived from the East in 871 AD. Viking reinforcements from Scandinavia landed in the shape of the "Great Summer Army". Under the command of Guthrum, Oscetel and Anwend they made their way up the Thames to Reading where they joined Halfdan. In May Alfred tried to gain a decisive defeat against the invaders at the Battle of Wilton. The encounter was another hard fought contest. According to the Anglo-Saxon chronicle Alfred's army was greatly outnumbered:

"With few and unequal forces Alfred met the invaders on the hill at Wilton"

Alfred gained the upper hand at first; the Danes seemed to have fallen back, but then Halfdan counterattacked with the Viking reserves and forced Alfred's men onto the back foot. As the Viking berserkers pushed the Saxon shield wall back the spirit of the Wessex men finally broke, leaving Halfdan in control of **"the field of carnage"**.

The nine battles and numerous skirmishes fought in the cold bleak winter and early spring of 870/871 AD had inflicted horrendous loses on both the West Saxons and their Viking counterparts. Since landing back in 865 AD the Vikings had not known such dogged and stubborn resistance. Within less than six months they had lost at least one King and countless Jarls. These loses affected the army's ability to remain together as a cohesive fighting unit. Only the strong command of the Ragnarsson brothers stopped the army from breaking up into disarray.

Wessex too had being badly bludgeoned during the campaign; its manpower resources had been decimated and its ability to function as a state had been tested to its very limits.

Alfred offered terms of an armistice which Halfdan and the other Viking commanders gladly agreed to. Some sort of Danegeld was offered on the condition that they left Wessex soil immediately. During the summer, the Vikings broke camp and headed for the Mercian city of London where they over wintered. Coins were minted in London during the winter of 871 AD bearing the name Halfdan, identifying him as the main Viking warlord of the Great Heathen Army. Any thoughts of returning to battle the West Saxons were put on hold when news reached London that the Northumbrian puppet King Egbert and the quisling Archbishop of York (Wulfhere) had been overthrown and forced to flee York. Strangely they were given refuge and asylum by King Burgred of Merica in a possible act of appeasement towards Great Heathen Army. Halfdan marshaled his troops and marched north to put down the revolt.

By the winter of 872 AD the army had crossed the River Trent and was encamped at Torksey. With the West Saxons still recovering from the 870-871 AD campaign and Mercia under the ineffectual leadership of King Bergred, Halfdan was free the deal with the rebellious Northumbrians. Over the next year he mercilessly destroyed all resistance against Viking rule in the North.

The Conquest of Mercia 873 - 874 AD

With Northern England now pacified, Halfdan turned his attention towards Mercia. King Burgred had been paying off the Vikings with the "Danegeld" in return for peace, but this policy was now regarded as a sign of weakness. Burgred had not helped the West Saxons in their hour of need and Halfdan knew Wessex was not strong enough to help Mercia if he invaded.

The heathens crossed into Mercia and set up a fortified position at Repton in Derbyshire. From there they ravaged the Middle Saxon Kingdom. Town after town fell to the Vikings and within months Burgred lost complete control and authority. The Mercian King fled into exile and left his people to fend for themselves. It was a shocking act of cowardice and dereliction of his duty as King. The Anglo-Saxon chronicle reported that:

"They drove King Burgred out of his Kingdom which he had reigned over for about 22 winters, and subdued all the land. He went to Rome where he remained for the rest of his life"

Mercia had fallen far easier than expected; Halfdan continued Ivar's policy of installing a puppet King on his newly acquired conquest. Ceowulf, one of the former King's Thanes was chosen to rule over Mercia. He gave hostages over to Halfdan and swore an oath of fealty.

The army splits and the Viking Kingdom of Jorvik

In less than ten years the Great Heathen Army had extinguished the Anglo-Saxon Kingdoms of Northumbria, East Anglia and Merica. Only Wessex lay between them and the total domination of the Southern part of the Island of Britannia.

In 875 AD Halfdan, Ubba, Guthrum and the other Viking leaders made a monumental decision at their camp in Repton (Derbyshire) to split up the army. Archeological evidence unearthed at Repton in the 1980s revealed a possible clue to the disbandment of the army.

Professor Martin and Birthe Biddle rediscovered an elaborate Pagan Viking burial in the grounds of St Wystan's church.

St Wystan's Church (Repton) location of the Great Heathen army's fortified encampment

Previously unearthed by a labourer in the 1600s who found "The remains of a human giant nine foot tall, and around it lay one hundred human skeletons, with their feet pointing towards the stone coffin" The Biddles re-excavation confirmed the original story of the labourer. At least 260 bodies were placed around the central corpse, who must have been a significant figure to the Great Heathen Army.

The only person of great stature who died during this period was Ivar "the Boneless". His body may have been brought over from Ireland to rest with the dead soldiers of the Great Heathen Army encamped at Repton. Ivar had always been regarded as the head of the army and his death may have brought an end its central cohesion.

Ragnar Lodbrok Saga:

"Ivar ruled over England until his dying day, when he became deathly sick, and when he lay with that killing–illness, he said that he should be moved to that place which was most exposed to raiding, and he said that he expected that anyone who landed there would gain no victory"

Possibly without Ivar's leadership and direction the sub commanders were free to pursue their own interests and objectives. After Ivar's death Halfdan decided to settle Northern Mercia and Northumbria with the older veterans of the army and those who wanted to exchange the sword for the plough, creating the Kingdom of Jorvik. Eager to show the Northumbrians of his right to rule, he first marched to the far north of the region over the river Tyne near modern day Newcastle, where he set up a base to launch a series of minor campaigns and raids to subdue the Picts and Strathclyde Britons.

These campaigns helped him win over the hearts and minds of the Northumbrians and also define the Kingdom of Jorvik's Northern frontier.

Anglo-Saxon Chronicle:
"He shared out the land of the Northumbrians between himself and his men, and his army was soon ploughing the land and living off it"

On returning from his successful campaign in the North Halfdan was crowned Halfdan I "King of Jorvik". Jorvik became one of the lost important settlements in the Viking world. Amber from the Baltic, walrus ivory and slaves were all traded in the bustling streets of the Northern capital. The city also became a central hub and manufacturing centre.

Reconstructed street of Viking age York, Jorvik Viking Centre, York, England

The name of Coppergate Street in York derives from Old Norse meaning "Street of the cup makers". Excavations around the location of the current Jorvik Viking centre have revealed that the city's Viking craftsmen were mass producing everyday artefacts such as combs shoes and pots. For nearly the next 100 years Jorvik remained the bastion of Viking power in England.

The end of Halfdan in Ireland 877 AD

Not content in just ruling Jorvik, Halfdan as Ivar's heir apparent claimed the title "King of Dublin". Gathering together a large war band he crossed the Irish Sea and deceitfully murdered Eyestein (Olaf the White's son). After the murder of Eyestein, Halfdan sat uneasy on the throne of Dublin. At a banquet he survived an assassination attempt upon his life by some disgruntled Viking and Irish nobles. Unable to control or trust the waring factions Halfdan abandoned Dublin and returned to the Kingdom of Jorvik, where he recruited soldiers and mercenaries to punish the Viking rebels in Ireland. Once back on Irish soil Halfdan conducted a final vengeful campaign of terror. In 877 AD he fought against a coalition of rebel forces (some of whom included Eyestein relatives) near Strangford Lough, Northern Ireland (*Strangr-fjörðr*) meaning "strong sea-inlet" in Old Norse. In the vicious battle that ensured Halfdan was slain in the fighting. His death ended the Ragnarssons direct link to the claim of the Kingdom of Dublin. Also in Jorvik a period "interregnum" descended upon the Norse Kingdom until Guthred was proclaimed King in 883 AD.

Halfdan I "King of Jorvik"

THE VIKING RULERS OF

866 JORVIK 954

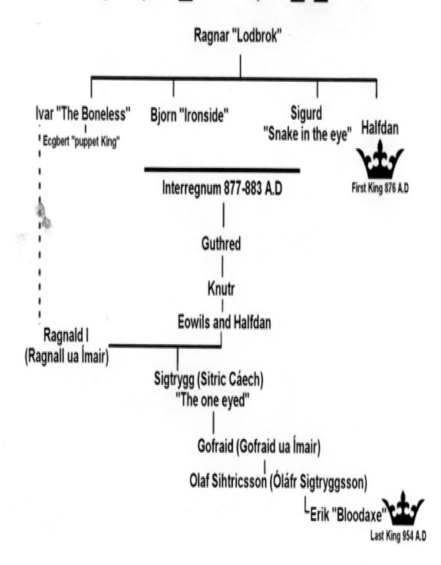

Ragnar "Lodbrok"

Ivar "The Boneless"

Ecgbert "puppet King"

Bjorn "Ironside"

Sigurd "Snake in the eye"

Halfdan

First King 876 A.D

Interregnum 877-883 A.D

Guthred

Knutr

Eowils and Halfdan

Ragnald I (Ragnall ua Ímair)

Sigtrygg (Sitric Cáech) "The one eyed"

Gofraid (Gofraid ua Ímair)

Olaf Sihtricsson (Óláfr Sigtryggsson)

Erik "Bloodaxe"

Last King 954 A.D

The last campaign of the Great Heathen Army

When the news of the separation of the Great Heathen Army reached the court of King Alfred in Wessex, the West Saxons breathed a sigh of relief, but this euphoria was abruptly shattered in 876 AD when Guthrum, now nominal leader of the Southern contingent of the Great Heathen Army burst out from the Viking camp at Cambridge and invaded Wessex.

Statue of King Alfred, Wantage, England

The campaign of 870-871 AD had been conducted along the River Thames which was the traditional border between Wessex and Merica. As a result much of the Wessex heartlands had been untouched by the fighting. Guthrum planned to take the war directly to the heart of Wessex and undermine Alfred's ability to protect his people. In a blitzkrieg attack under the cover of darkness the Viking army dashed out of their base in Cambridge and advanced straight across Wessex, deep into the Kingdom.

The West Saxons were taken by complete surprise and were unable to stop Guthrum's men setting up a defensive position at Wareham on the Wessex coastline. When Alfred's Fryd arrived at Wareham it became clear that an attack on the Viking fortifications would be out of the question, remembering the debacle of the failed assault on Halfdan's camp at Reading in 871 AD. The Vikings stationed their longships on Brownsea Island, thus protecting the entrance to the harbour at Poole and also keeping them out of the way from any would-be Saxon attack.

With no other course of action left open to him King Alfred negotiated with Guthrum and offered him the Danegeld to leave. The King made Guthrum swear an oath on the

Wyvern banner of Wessex

holy ring of Thor. By choosing a pagan relic Alfred hoped Guthrum would keep his word. The Viking leader had other ideas and under the cover of darkness he murdered the West Saxon hostages who had been exchanged during the negotiations and struck camp. He headed deeper into Wessex, heading for the old Roman town of Exeter (Isca Dvmnoniorvm). Alfred had been duped and outwitted, he tried to pursue the Vikings, but by the time he caught up with them they had already reached Exeter.

More bad news followed when his scouts brought back word that a huge Viking fleet was sailing around the South coast to join up with Guthrum's force. Alfred knew that if these forces joined together the Kingdom of Wessex would be doomed. Only divine intervention could save Wessex now, but luck was on the West Saxons side when a storm scattered and destroyed the Viking fleet in the Channel. Although the Viking reinforcements had been destroyed, Alfred was still not strong enough to eject the Viking host from Exeter. Instead a stalemate ensued, Guthrum held out until the harvest time. He knew full well that Alfred could not keep the Saxon fryd in the field during this important period. Negotiations led to another uneasy truce, allowing Guthrum to remain at Exeter over the winter.

This time Guthrum kept his word and left Wessex in the summer of 877 AD. He returned over the border to Mercia and stationed the army at Gloucester. Alfred suspicious of Guthrum's activity set up his court at Chippenham close to the Mercian border. Learning from Ivar and Halfdan, Guthrum decided to surprise the West Saxons by launching an attack on the Christian holiday on the 6th of January (Twelfth night). It was a masterstroke, as Alfred and his court were reveling and celebrating the religious festivities, the Great Heathen Army advanced through the snow covered landscape towards the Royal manor. On reaching Chippenham they quickly overwhelmed the Royal bodyguards and rampaged through the streets looking for King Alfred. The King, his wife Elswitha and his young children only just managed to escape the carnage into the darkness. Alfred was forced to flee to the safety of the Isle of Athelney in the Somerset marshes to avoid capture.

GUTHRUM

Guthrum tried to convince the West Saxons that King Alfred had abandoned his people just like King Burgred had done with the Mercians, but while Alfred was still alive he could not place a puppet on the throne of Wessex. From his base in Somerset King Alfred spread the word that he was still alive as urged his compatriots to join him and fight a guerilla war against the invaders.

The death of Ubba and the last battle 878 AD

During the Viking campaign to subdue Wessex, Guthrum called upon one of the original commanders of the Great Heathen Army for assistance. Ubba, last of the Ragnarsson sons answered the call to arms and sailed with his Viking fleet from Dyfed in South Wales towards Devon. The objective of the two separate Viking armies was to corner Alfred in a two pronged attack.

As Ubba marched east to link up with Guthrum, his force was confronted by Odda and the Devonshire Fryd near the old fortress of Arx Cynuit (disputed location in North Devon).

Ubba surrounded the stronghold and planned to force the garrison to surrender due to the fortress having no supply of fresh water, but Odda and his men had decided to attack first. Calmly waiting until the break of dawn, he launched a formidable attack on the Viking besiegers. The West Saxons stormed out of the defensive ringworks and smashed straight into the Ubba's unprepared Viking lines, heading straight for the sacred raven banner.

Caught completely by surprise, the Vikings were overrun and annihilated. Ubba fought on to the bitter end, fighting to protect his father's talisman, but it was in vain as he was finally overwhelmed and cut down. The survivors fled in terror back to their ships with Ubba's body. Later sources allege that the battle took place in a wood called "bois de pene". The sacred Odin raven banner which was said to flutter its wings before a victory and hang limp before a defeat was captured by the victorious Devonshire men. The flag was steeped in legend and was said to have been made by Ubba's three sisters as a present to their father Ragnar Lodbrok "Hairy breaches".

The Anglo-Saxon chronicle reported that:

"The brother of Ivar and Halfdan landed in Devonshire with 23 ships. He was slain along with 840 of troops and the men of Devon captured his war flag called the Raven"

Ubba's body may have taken to the safe haven of Lundy Island (Puffin Island in Old Norse) in the middle of the St Georges Channel where it was buried. Local legend recounts that a pagan burial was uncovered revealing a skeleton of an eight foot tall giant, believed to be that of Ubba. (The Giant's grave). The death of Ubba also signaled the end of the Heathen Army's campaign. The pincer strategy had failed and it was Alfred who took the initiative in the spring of 878 AD. Galvanized by the defeat of Ubba's Vikings in Devon, he ventured out from hiding in the Somerset levels and rallied the West Saxons for the final showdown with the remnants of the Great Heathen Army.

Lundy Island, meaning Puffin Island in Old Norse possible last resting place of Ubba Ragnarsson

The Battle of Edington 878 AD

At a place called Ecgbryhtesstan (Egbert's Stone) Alfred mustered the Anglo-Saxon army. The men of Wilshire, Somerset, Devon, Hampshire and all the free lands of the English gathered behind the Wyvern banner of Wessex to fight for Alfred and the destiny and future of the Island of Britannia. Defeat was unthinkable and this was the last throw of the dice for the Anglo-Saxons. At Edington in Wiltshire near Bratton camp Alfred's army squared up against the invaders. The Anglo-Saxon's proudly brandished Ragnar's captured raven banner and taunted the Vikings with their battle cry "Out, Out, Out".

The death of Ubba Ragnarsson

Alfred formed his army into a shield wall and advanced towards the Vikings. Leading from the front he fought bravely, hacking through the enemy ranks. Fighting like a wild boar he forced the heathens to abandon the field and retreat.

The battle ended in a total victory for King Alfred and the Anglo-Saxons, Edington marked the end of the Great Heathen Army's 14 year reign of terror.

"Fighting ferociously, forming a dense shield-wall against the whole army of the Pagans, and striving long and bravely...at last he gained victory. He overthrew the Pagans with great slaughter, and smiting the fugitives, he pursued them as far as the fortress of Chippenham."

The Great Heathen army had been smashed once and for all, the survivors fled back to Chippenham where they hoped to re-group and wait for the harvest. Alfred at once ordered his army to strip the surrounding area of its food resources and provisions.

He was determined to force the remaining Vikings

The memorial stone commemorating the Battle of Ethandun (Edington) 878 AD

to surrender before the harvest of 878 AD. Unable to breakout or pillage the local region, Guthrum's situation was bleak. Inside the wooden stockade of Chippenham the Vikings were cold, hungry and many of them desperately wounded. After two weeks of holding out, Guthrum had no choice but to seek terms of surrender.

Bishop Asser:
"The heathens terrified by hunger, cold and fear, begged for peace"

At first he sent word to King Alfred that he would offer hostages in return for a safe passage out of Wessex, but Alfred refused knowing the plight of the Vikings inside the fortress. Magnanimous in victory Alfred offered to spare Guthrum and his remaining soldiers if he and his men agree to convert to Christianity. They would then be allowed to return to East Anglia unmolested.

King Alfred with the Viking warlord Guthrum

Guthrum was astounded by the offer and agreed immediately. Taking the Christian name Athelstan he was baptised in the presence of his new godfather King Alfred. For the next twelve days Alfred entertained Guthrum, now Athelstan and the senior Viking commanders.

After the festivities, Guthrum disbanded the Great Heathen Army and returned to East Anglia where he ruled as King. He kept his word as a man of honour and remained loyal to Alfred until his death in 890 AD.

The Treaty of Wedmore

At the Treaty of Wedmore King Alfred and Guthrum agreed to a permanent peace. Alfred knew the survival of Wessex and indeed his people "the English" would require all his skills of Kingship. Although he had defeated the Great Heathen Army and had earned the respect and loyalty of Guthrum, the threat from other Viking warlords from Scandinavia and beyond remained the greatest concern to Anglo-Saxon England.

Alfred overhauled the English Fryd. He introduced a Rota system into the Fryd where half the men from an Earldom could be called up for service, leaving the other half to attend to the crops and harvest. The King had also learned from the tactics of the Great Heathen Army. He saw no reason why the English could not copy the Vikings in using fortifications as a base during a campaign. Selected towns or villages, sometimes using old Roman defensive walls within 20 miles of each other were converted into a "Burgh" (fortified settlement). This meant that if the Vikings attacked, the local inhabitants could retreat into the nearest burgh and defend themselves until the Anglo-Saxon Fryd/field army arrived.

This new system paid dividends when a Viking raiding fleet attacked Rochester in 885 AD.

The Anglo-Saxon chronicle:

"They besieged the city and made fortifications around themselves, but the English defended the City until King Alfred arrived with his army. The invaders abandoned their position and set back across the sea"

Following up the victory over the Viking invasion force of 885 AD Alfred captured the Mercian City of London which lay under the control of the Guthrum's Viking East Anglians. In order to diffuse the strained peace with Guthrum Alfred turned over the city to the leader of the free Mercians Ealdorman Ethelred.

The King then drew up an official Treaty with Guthrum to define the frontiers of Anglo-Saxon England and the Viking controlled territories.

Viking attack on an Anglo-Saxon "Burh"

866

Rock of Dumbarton

Strathclyde

English
Northumbria

Southern Britain
880 AD
— — — —
Danelaw Frontier between
Anglo-Saxon England and
the Viking controlled North

Kingdom of
York

Jorvik

Dublin

Chester

The Danelaw

Wales

English
Mercia

East
Anglia

London

Wessex

Winchester

954

The old Roman road of Watling Street running from London in the south to Chester in the north was chosen as a rough boundary. Using Watling Street and the river boundaries of the Thames, the River Lea and the Ouse the border was defined. The lands north of the frontier became known as the "Danelaw". One of the most important aspects of the Treaty was the "Wergild". This clause allowed both English and Danish/Viking subjects to be treated on equal terms within the two separate Kingdoms. If a Danish subject killed and Englishman or visa-versa the guilty party would have to pay the "Wergild" compensation money to the relatives of the slain. The Treaty bore its fruits and slowly over time many of the Danes became assimilated into the English race.

Hastein's war 892 – 894 AD

King Guthrum died in 890 AD and his death sparked another attempted Viking invasion, this time by the warlord Hastein. Hastein had been one of the chieftains who had accompanied Bjorn "Ironside" and the Ragnarsson brothers on the famous Mediterranean raid (859-862 AD). After the raid Hastein settled in Brittany and forged an uneasy alliance with Duke Salomon. Together they defeated the Franks at the Battle of Brissarthe (near Chateauneauf sur Sarthe) in which they killed Robert "the Strong" (Marquis of the Marches of Neustria) and Ranulf I Duke of Aquitaine. Over the next 20 years Hastein ravaged modern day North Western France, sacking Angers, Orleans, Bourges and Tours. The Norman chronicler Dudo de St Quentin described him as amongst other things as an extremely cruel double dealing hypocrite. Upon the death of King Guthrum and the stiffening of resistance on the continent Hastein decided to launch an invasion of Wessex. Hastein landed his force at Milton (near Sittingbourne) of the Kentish coast. A second force arrived and set up a fortified base at Appledore on the estuary of the river Lympe. Alfred at once raised the Fryd army and positioned himself between the two armies, stopping them from uniting together. Under constant pressure and unable to raid the local vicinity Hastein agreed to terms. His two sons were baptised and like Guthrum before King Alfred became their Godfather along with Ealdorman Ethelred of Mercia. Hastein abandoned Milton and crossed the Thames where he constructed a new fortification at Benfleet (Essex). During the Easter celebrations of 893 AD the Appledore Vikings broke camp and tried the force their way deeper into Wessex. At Farnham they were intercepted by Aflred's son Prince Edward. Taken by the speed and surprise of Prince Edward's men the Vikings were routed and forced to retreat. The survivors made there way to Thorney Island where they sought terms of surrender. Prince Edward agreed to allow the survivors to go free, under the condition they give hostages and leave Wessex immediately.

No sooner than the Viking threat in Kent had been dispersed, another appeared out of the blue. The Danelaw Vikings of the Kingdom of Jorvik and East Anglia had raised a fleet of over 100 ships and attacked Devon, hoping to take advantage of the English Fryd's involvement in containing the Vikings in Eastern Wessex. King Alfred realised the danger of being caught in a pincer movement, just as Guthrum and Ubba had tried to do back in 878 AD. Prince Edward and Ealdorman Ethelred were immediately dispatched to destroy Hastein's lair at Benfleet, while the King marched west to confront the Danelaw Vikings. After raising extra troops from London the Princes army surrounded the Viking fortification at Benfleet. When they obtained information that Hastein and the main Viking force were not inside the fort, Edward and Ethelred decided to attack and used their superior numbers to overwhelm the defenders.

Anglo Saxon Chronicle:
"They put the army to flight, stormed the fort and took all that there was within, goods as well as women and children. All their ships were either broke up into pieces, burnt or brought back to London and Rochester"

Hastein's wife and sons were captured in the retaliatory raid on Benfleet. They were taken to King Alfred who magnanimously had them returned to Hastein. The old warlord had regrouped and constructed another camp at Shoebury some 15 miles east of Benfleet. Hastein may have relinquished command of the army upon the return of his wife and children for he disappears from the records of the Anglo Saxon chronicle. Meanwhile in the West Country Alfred had forced the Danelaw Vikings to abandon the siege of Exeter and Countisbury. The remnants of the raiding fleet tried to attack Chichester, but beneath the formidable Roman walls they were driven off and slaughtered by the English garrison.

Although defeated, the Vikings were not yet ready to give up the fight against the English. At Shoebury Hastein's force was replenished with new recruits from the Danelaw Kingdoms. In a daring raid they (possibly under Hastein's command) sailed down the Thames estuary heading west. They may have been unaware of the Viking defeat in Devon and were possibly still hoping to join up with them.

On the English Welsh border they fortified themselves at Buttington (near Welshpool) where Offa's Dyke meets the river Seven, but a combined force of English and Welshmen besieged their encampment. According to the Anglo Saxon Chronicle:

"After many weeks had passed, some of the heathen died of hunger, but some, having by then eaten their horses, broke out of the fortress, and joined battle with those who were on the east bank of the river. But, when many thousands of pagans had been slain, and all the others had been put to flight, the Christians were masters of the place of death. In that battle the most noble Ordheah and many of the King's thegns were killed."

After Buttington and a further defeat whilst trying to occupy the old Roman Legionary fortress at Chester, the first Viking war peered out. King Alfred had saved Wessex and laid the foundations for the unification and creation of the nation state of England. His heirs would go on to crush the Viking menace and re-conquer the Danelaw. As for the Vikings they would return, but that is another story in itself.

Also Available:

THE PAGAN LORDS

The forgotten Viking campaigns of the Great Heathen Army in France and Spain 840 – 982 AD

Other titles in the series
"The Normans"

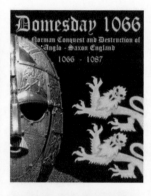

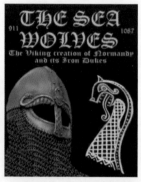

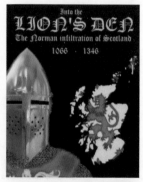

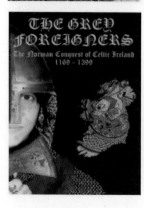

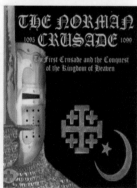

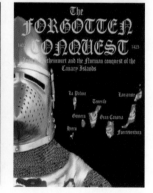

Printed in Great Britain
by Amazon